THE PAIN
BEHIND MY SMILE

THE PAIN BEHIND MY SMILE

Unveiling My Mask

ADRIENNE LOGAN

ISBN: 1545535868
ISBN 13: 9781545535868

TABLE OF CONTENTS

INTRODUCTION

Looking back over my life, I have been through a lot, and I have seen a lot. I have learned to take the good with the bad and not complain about the things I cannot change. In life, you experience things for a reason. Whether you are not in that place at that moment to understand it, or it comes to you later as you mature, for the most part, your experiences make and mold you into the person you are and the person you will become. I have endured so much pain and grief in my life I have become numb to showing feelings, and having emotions. I automatically expect the worst of people, so if they cross me or let me down, I am not devastated.

I am a woman with a good heart, and I will let no one else's hang-ups and insecurities change me. I am who I am, and I stand for what is right. I know my self-worth and what I have to offer to this world.

ACKNOWLEDGEMENTS

I would like to give an honor to God through whom all blessings flow. Next, I would like to thank my children for trusting and believing in me. To everyone that impacted my life good or bad, you helped to make me who I am. A special thanks to a special friend of mine, Tyrone, that saw me at an early age hanging with the wrong crowd and pulled me aside and said, "I don't like what I am seeing, this is not you. You don't look right hanging with the people that your hanging with." I reflected on the conversation we had for about a month. I took your advice and went back to my parent's house and regrouped and came up with my life's plan. What you saw in me back then, put me on track and I am forever grateful.

To my photographer, Rossie Martin, RMartin
Photos, I thank you for your talented work.
Thank You

FAMILY FIRST

I was born in Wilmington DE in the early 70's. The earliest memories I have is when I was 4 years old. I recall, my parents taking my siblings and me to the site where our family home had just been built. There were still huge piles of dirt left over that was bulldozed out of the way. We would run and play on the dirt hills and have a ball. We all took turns posing on top of the dirt mounds, while my mom took our pictures. She pulled out her big black Polaroid instant camera and snapped away. Our home was a fresh new green 4-bedroom rancher with a full basement. We had a lot of land and woods behind our home with adventurous trails. My mother was a stay at home mom, and my dad worked for a major car manufacturer. Buying a home for the first time was a major accomplishment for minorities in that era.

My name is Adrienne, and I am the youngest of five. I have 3 older brothers and 1 older sister. In order from oldest to youngest, there are Thomas, Ann, William, Douglas, and me. Since I was the youngest, I didn't have many childhood memories of Thomas and Ann. The reason is there was a 10-year difference between Thomas and me, and an 8-year difference between Ann and me. What I knew is that my oldest brother, Thomas, was a mild-mannered person. He was brown-skinned, with a medium build, and average height. Thomas stayed to himself and was quiet, but when you pushed his buttons, he had the potential to snap. I recollect my middle brother, William, sneaking into Thomas's room without permission. Thomas was outside taking out the garbage, and William went into his room to borrow something. Thomas had come back inside without William hearing him. Thomas strolled down the hallway and turned the corner to enter his room. To his surprise, there stood William snooping around. Thomas snatched William up by his shirt and pinned him against the wall with his feet dangling in the air. You could see the fear in William's watery eyes. Thomas yelled, "I told you to stay out of my room!" and dropped William. William slid down the wall covered with Jet Magazine's Beauty's of the Week.   This was the first time I saw the other side of my oldest brother.   A few years later, Thomas graduated and enlisted in the United States Military.   He made a career of it and never returned home.

My sister Ann was the mischievous one.   Ann was short, dark skinned, and fully developed.   She was hot tempered, and always ready to fight.   Ann was advanced for her age and was always down to try new things.   She didn't care if it would get her in trouble.   At the age of 13, Ann would steal a few cigarettes out of our father's cigarette pack he kept on the kitchen table.   Ann would wait until our parents went to bed and go outside and smoke.   By 14 or 15, she discovered boys, and that's when she went out of control. She snuck out at night, skipped school, and other various delinquent activities.   Ann and I shared a bedroom, so I would observe her doing a lot of things.   One night I was in bed, and Ann was sitting on the floor next to the bed talking on the phone.   I went to sleep.   In the middle of the night, I awoke and saw her gathering clothes.   I looked at her and she yelled at me and told me to go back to sleep. I obeyed.   The next morning, I woke up to the weeping of my mother.   She had found the note Ann had left on the kitchen table, informing my parents she had run away.

All teenagers can't wait to be grown and get out in the world. The reality of it is there is no place like home. After being gone for one day,

Ann's best friend's parents called our house to let my parents know Ann was there. My parents rushed and picked her up and brought her home. Deep down inside, Ann was happy to be home. She took a hot shower and ate my mother's home cooked Chicken and Dumplings. As a family, we put all that behind us, and the next day was a new day. William was my middle brother, and he was a gamester. He was drawn to anything dealing with gambling. As a young lad, he knew how to play deuces, pity pat, tonk, and poker. William would enter the grown-up card games playing for real money. There was a time he won hundreds of dollars from my aunts and uncles playing poker. With his winnings, he could buy his own school clothes and some fly new kicks.

Now, it brings me to my youngest brother, Douglas. Douglas and I were closer in age, so we played and did childlike things together. Douglas wore brown, thick glasses with tape on the left arm. He was chocolate and pudgy. His personality was laid back and he went with the flow. He chose not to hang with a lot of people and to just hang with William. Douglas was a diehard wrestling fan. Each Saturday morning, he would watch the WWF Wrestling. When the episode went off, the two of us would go outside. That's when he would practice everything he learned on me. Week after week, I would go inside crying to my mom, after Douglas practiced his amateur wrestling moves on me. Did I learn my lesson? No, I was just over-joyed he was spending time with me. Richie Rich was our pet German Sheppard. My best friend, LaTanya, gave him to me in kindergarten when her dog had puppies. I named him Richie Rich because that was my favorite cartoon. Richie grew quickly into a brave burly dog. He became part of our family and was loved by all of us. Richie was very loyal and protective. I even begged my dad to build him a dog house with the dollar sign on it to be exactly like the cartoon. With this sweet innocent face, how could Daddy tell me no.

STUTTER STUTTER

Growing up in a small suburban town may be boring as a kid. It appears there was never anything to do, and no other kids to do it with, since the next neighbor lived a half of a mile away. Also, when you are a frail girl with nappy hair, it made it even harder to fit in. As a child, I was always quiet and smiled all the time. Adults always complemented me and would say I had such a beautiful smile. I stayed in a happy mood for a child; only my immediate family knew why I smiled so much. Until the age of 11, I had a secret I was harboring. I didn't talk because I had a stuttering problem, which made me afraid to speak. This made me stay in my comfort zone and just smile and say the bare minimum. This logic had gotten me by, until one Tuesday morning in Mrs. Brown's reading class, things changed. I had just entered the 3rd grade and Mrs. Brown was my reading teacher. She was a very attractive young Afro-American woman with a very sleek style of dress. She would wear a variety of tailored pant suits and would add a designer bag on her arm for a little more pizazz. I noticed she would add a hint of eyeshadow and lipstick to make her outfit complete. She loved her job and all her students, and would go above and beyond for each one of them. We had a great group of students in our class. My two best friends, Carlise and LaTanya, were in my class, and we were inseparable. We rode the school bus together, all of us lived in the country, and we would sit on the phone for hours every night and figure out what we were wearing the next day. Carlise was short and good-humored, while LaTanya was tall for her age, outspoken, and ready for whatever came her way. She was the wrong person to mess with. Every class has a bully, and our class had Josh Wiggins! Josh was a short, obese white boy that always had something smart or negative to say. He was known for mimicking all the other students when they would talk or read. He would make the other students do his assignments, and if they didn't comply, he threatened to break their faces.

I constantly had butterflies zooming around in my stomach each day I entered her class. The thought of being put on the spot and humiliated terrified me. So, when Mrs. Brown called on me to read the second paragraph out loud to the class, that started the beginning of the worst day of my life as I had known it! I took a deep breath and began to read slowly and carefully. My hands clammed up, and, I felt the sweat dripping from my armpits. I was doing good for a while, until I suddenly hit the word MOMENT in the sentence, and I got scared. For me, the letter M gave me difficulties. I closed my eyes for a split second and took a short sigh, then fixed my mouth to form the M sound. It came out m-m-mo-mo- moment. The class sat in complete silence. Suddenly, Josh Wiggins burst out laughing hysterically and said, "Are you d-d-d- DONE!!!!????"

My face turned from brown to red instantly. Mrs. Brown yelled at Josh and kicked him out of the class for being so rude. Carlise and LaTanya turned around and stared at me as if they were watching me drown, but couldn't help me because they couldn't swim. Mrs. Brown stood up and apologized to me and began to explain to the class what stuttering was. She told the class that stuttering could be corrected if I learned how to relax, and did not get nervous, and took my time. My classmates had no problem with it, and ironically, they embraced my friendship even more after that. When class dismissed, Mrs. Brown kept me after class and wrote a note for me to give to my mother. The note explained what happened in class and a name and number of a doctor she thought would help me.

Two weeks later, I had my appointment with the speech doctor. He seemed to be a nice older gentleman with thick glasses, and his name was Dr. Rottenburgh. While he talked, and explained things to me, he would blink a lot, and his left hand would shake vigorously. He made me do different speech tests by saying crazy words and enunciating them. The techniques he taught me were a little silly at first, but they were helpful. I was first taught to relax my mind and body before speaking. Next, I had to practice talking to myself in the mirror. I did this every night to rebuild my confidence. Also, I had to read books out loud, which helped me to breathe correctly. To his findings, my condition was minor and fixable. We did a few sessions each month of the speech exercises to determine if it helped me. After 6 weeks, Dr. Rottenburgh released me from his care, because he noticed improvement. He sent me home with a few books to read to help me pronounce words, but overall, he said take your time; you are causing yourself to experience anxiety, so when you speak, your words are coming out wrong. He instructed me to breathe and take my time, and I would be fine. When I left Dr. Rottenberg's office that day, I worked hard to get better. I read the books he gave me and developed a habit to want to read just because. I read harder books with bigger and harder words to show off to my class. This rebuilt my confidence, and in no time, I became a new person. After a few months, my classmates were fed up with Josh's threats and told Mrs. Brown he made the other kids in the class do his work. To put an end to his bullying, Mrs. Brown gave Josh his own assignments different from the rest of the class. She even sent him out of the class on test day to sit in the principal's office and take his test supervised.

Throughout the rest of the school year, I continued to improve and stayed focus on growing. On our last day of school, Mrs. Brown threw the class a party for all of our hard work. We had a lot of treats, like Vanilla and Chocolate Ice Cream Cups, Rice Krispy Treats, and homemade Peanut Butter Hershey Kiss Cookies. As the party came to an end, Mrs. Brown handed out the final report cards. You could hear the students talking among one another and telling each other their grade. As Mrs. Brown got to Josh and handed him his report card, he was quiet. He hurriedly put his report card in his backpack without even viewing it. I heard Mrs. Brown say in a sarcastic way, "You already know what you got. Hopefully, you will do better in my class next year." Carlise, LaTanya, and I all looked at one another and gave each other a smirk. I was glad he stayed back in third grade for the way he humiliated me that day when I was reading. Before we left to start our summer vacation, Mrs. Brown said she had one last thing to say. She said she had a student in her class she wanted to recognize for their achievements throughout the year and how they improved. She then said, "I would like to present this Certificate of Most Improved Student to Adrienne Logan." I was surprised! Carlise and LaTanya clapped and then everyone else joined in. Josh sat there speechless. I walked gracefully up to the front of the classroom to receive my certificate. On the way, back to my seat, I rolled my eyes at Josh and took my seat.   Mrs. Brown officially dismissed the class, and our summer began. As Carlise, LaTanya, and I got on the school bus to go home, we talked about Josh and how he failed the third grade, and how it was so deserving of him. No one took the time to get to know him nor did he allow anyone to get close to him. His life was always such a mystery. Over our summer break, I recall hearing the news broadcast one night on television with a breaking story. The news reporter told the viewers about two young boys drowning in our local lake. The two boys' bodies were recovered, but their names were not being released until the family was notified. The next morning, as I ate my cereal at the kitchen table, my mother read the daily newspaper. She asked me if I knew the boys that drowned the night before. I told her when I saw the news they didn't reveal the name. Next, my mother said, "Well, it says right here the two swimmers were later identified as 9-year-old Josh Wiggins and his 11-year-old cousin William Wiggins."

I was crushed. I ran to the phone and called LaTanya. I asked her if she heard about Josh, and she said she had just found out too. Carlise was away at camp, so we could not reach her. When the story unfolded, some said Josh and his cousin ignored the no swimming signs, and when nightfall had settled in, they snuck out of the house and went swimming. To their dismay, the current was way to strong and quickly took both young men under. William was visiting Josh from Virginia for the summer. Reporters said, when Josh's mother went to his bedroom to check on them for the evening, she noticed they were gone. Josh's parents rode around the neighborhood and didn't find the boys. They drove to the lake and found the two boys' backpacks and Josh's radio. The farmer that lived next to the lake came out of the house and said he had called the police, because two young boys were drinking and horse playing at the lake, and when he yelled to them, they jumped in the water. As they went out farther, they were over taken by the rough waters and went under.

No matter how obnoxious Josh was, I still felt sad that he was gone forever. The pain his parents and younger sister had to endure was much more hurtful than the embarrassment of him teasing me. I learned at a very young age that, despite the way someone treats you, never let them change the person you are.

DADDY DON'T
DRINK NO MORE

B eing the youngest of five siblings had its advantages. My mother was a stay at home mom, and my dad worked for Chrysler Corporation for 30 years. He perfected being a jack of all trades. My dad plowed and made our garden, fixed cars, cooked, fished, hunted and much more. By my father being the sole provider, he had to have an outlet to unwind, and his was drinking. When I arrived home from school and did my homework, my dad would be outside doing something around the house or sitting at the kitchen table with a Budweiser staringoutside the window and taking in God's creation. After a few hours, the transformation began from Jekyll to Hyde.

I observed early in life that my dad had a drinking problem, and it bothered me. I never wanted Carlise or LaTanya to come over to visit, or spend the night, because I knew it took little time before he got "fired up" and made a scene, and I didn't want to be the laughingstock of my school. Playing it safe, I went to their houses to avoid any mishaps, by my father being a drinker; on the weekends, my parents visited my aunt and uncle's house or my aunt and uncle visited our house. The grown-ups played cards, listened to music, ate, and socialized. The children played tag, red light green light, and kickball.

When my family from Baltimore came over to visit, it was always epic. My aunt RuthAnn and her husband, William, had 8 children, 7 daughters, and one son. Aunt RuthAnn was very sharp and stylish. She had that city flare with her, so whenever she came to visit, her Clothes and her hairdo were always a show stopper. She was short and easy going, but if you pushed her buttons, she knew how to get down and dirty quick. My Uncle William was a character. He was tall and light skinned and a suave dresser. Uncle William had a distinctive brown mole on his nose. I recall being a child and saying out loud, "Uncle William got a chocolate chip on his nose!" My parents gave me the look of death, because I had embarrassed them by my outburst.

Uncle William laughed it off and thought it was amusing. Uncle William would rarely talk normal English. He had his own language he made up and swore everyone else understood what he was saying. By now, everyone knew to agree with everything he said to keep the peace. My cousins were amazed by the country life, because they lived in the city. My one cousin's nickname was Puffy. She always showed us the latest dances and styles of dress, but her city accent became her trademark. She would get out of the car when they arrived to visit and say "Wait a minute, ya'll still got that dug?" We would giggle and say, "Yeah we still got that **dog** and it don't bite!" When nighttime fell upon us, all the girls would catch the lightning bugs and pull them apart and make earrings out of them. We ran around outside with our ears glowing in the dark, which became the coolest thing ever.

One weekend at our house, we had company over from several states. The grown-ups mingled as normal, when my dad and his cousin, Bernard, got into an argument. It got heated and escalated to both calling one another outside to fight. Family members tried to intervene, while others gathered around to see what was going to happen next. I became nervous, because I didn't want my dad to fight. The crazy thing about the whole situation was that the guy my dad was about to fight was blind and used a cane! I thought it was hilarious.

My grandparents were there, and my grandmother didn't want to see her son fight. My grandmother's name was Hattie-Mae, and my grandfather's name was Albert. Grandma Hattie was tall and frail with a nutmeg skin tone. She would always wear long skirts and knee-hi's. When she would come over on Sundays after church, she was known for giving out snacks to the children. Her trademark was when Grandma would sit down and go into her black Patten Leather purse and pull out a shiny piece of aluminum foil folded over. She would open the foil and inside was strawberry licorice sticks that she would hand out to all the grandchildren.

My Grandpa Albert was short and dark-skinned. He was very intelligent, and kept you on your toes by saying sly things to people. While the party was going on, my grandpa initiated a debate about the difference of being book smart and street smart. My grandpa then said, "Ok, I have something for ya'll." He asked for a piece of paper and wrote a math problem. The problem was as follows… 19-1=20. He instructed everyone in the kitchen to figure out this problem. After an hour of going back and forth and frustration, we all gave up. My grandpa took the paper and slowly and arrogantly wrote the roman numeral x, the roman numeral I, and the roman numeral x. He then erased the roman numeral I, and put the pencil down and smiled with a sinister grin, and took a sip of his Inver House Scotch. He was so tickled that he had outwitted everyone, and that made his day. So, that's when Grandma Hattie's protective instinct kicked in, and she staged a fake fainting spell to stop the madness and divert everyone's attention to her, to get my dad out of the fight. My grandma was sitting in the chair in the kitchen. She stood up, and suddenly, she plopped back down in her seat and fell back into the kitchen garbage can. Her skirt slightly came u, showing her famous nude knee-hi's gripping her skinny legs. Everyone ran back into the kitchen to see what was going on and to give assistance. My mother immediately called 911 to get help. The first responders quickly arrived on the scene. They took my grandma's vitals and talked to her to make sure she was coherent. When the E.M.T.'s were through with their evaluation, they took Grandma Hattie to the hospital for observations. She was released later that night with instructions to get plenty of rest. The creativity between both grandparents caused such a great diversion it put a halt on the initial fight. By now, it was almost midnight. My cousins still had a two-hour drive to get home. We kissed and hugged and said goodbye and safe travels, and they piled into the van. As Aunt RuthAnn pulled out of the drive way, Uncle William started yelling his crazy language out of the passenger side window. We all laughed and waved, as if we knew what he was saying and then the van was out of sight.

My dad and Cousin Bernard never fought. My grandmother survived, and the party continued. This was the norm for our family and the gatherings we held. These experiences led me to have only a social drink of wine or champagne, because I learned early how alcohol can alter a person's personality quickly. Even in my adulthood, meeting men that were heavy drinkers were a turn off to me. I was just so scarred from seeing how alcohol can make you act crazy, and I didn't want to have to deal with the altered personalities and the embarrassment.

SUMMERTIME

The year was 1992, and I had just graduated high school. I was 18, and "grown" and no one could tell me anything. I had originally planned on going into the United States Marine Corp, but eventually took a year off and just hung out before getting back to the grind. Most graduates got brand new cars for their achievements, but for me, that wasn't the case. My father handed me a yellow Ford Pinto with a blue primer fender. Without a doubt, it was an eyesore, but looking at the brighter side of things, it took me where I needed to go.

My cousin Rochelle and I were inseparable. Many people said we looked alike; she was just much taller than I was. Despite that fact we didn't have the best set of wheels, when Rochelle and I stepped out of the Pinto, our appearance made up for it. The two of us were two baby chicks that escaped the nest and were ready to see what life had in store for us. We would go to the mall every weekend to get an outfit for whatever party we were attending that weekend. One of our favorite outfits we had alike were these cross colored short sets with the matching jacket. Then we finished the look with a multicolor Asics tennis shoe.

While hanging out, Rochelle and I ran into 2 young guys that were twin brothers. Their names were Bryan and Ryan. The pair were short with hazel eyes. Bryan was very athletic and into all sports, while Ryan was more into music. Bryan wore his hair in long braids braided in many creative styles. Ryan had a close cut with his waves flowing all over so perfectly. Bryan and Ryan were from the streets, but they knew how to turn it on and off when they needed to. Rochelle and I became tight with the brothers, and they looked out for us. It was more of a brother-sister relationship between us all. We gained their trust and respect immediately. Where the brothers were from, they had parties every weekend at their local lodge. Anybody and everybody came out on those Saturday nights. It was interesting for Rochelle and me to see the street hustlers come out in the finest clothes and gold chains. They were pulling up in Audis and Lexus 400 Sedans with rims, with their car systems on blast. It was considered a baller's bash. When the parties would let out, everyone would just hang out on certain blocks and chill outside until 3 or 4 a.m.

The Skating Rink was another hang out Bryan and Ryan introduced us to. Sunday nights, people came from all around the Tri-State area Trenton, Philly, and Delaware to participate in this event. To keep out the riff-raff, the owner would walk the floor with a gigantic German Shepard on a leash. Everyone knew the owner was not for the nonsense, and he meant business. One night, as Rochelle, Bryan, Ryan, and I were skating to "They want to EFX" by Das EFX, a fight broke out between some out of town fellas. It was said that the young dude from Trenton was trying to talk to a young lady from Philly. The young lady's boyfriend didn't take to his advances well and snapped. He hit the Trenton dude in the head with a bottle and began punching him. When the young dude from Trenton fell on the floor, the Philly guy and his crew stomped him. There was extreme chaos! Everyone was running, screaming, and pushing. Some people got out, but the owner locked the door, so the people involved in the fight couldn't get away. He also let his dog out under his command to control the crowd. The State Troopers swiftly took over the scene. They began to mace people and arrest those involved in the confrontation. The four of us were stuck inside coughing and gagging from the pepper spray released. All our eyes were blazing. They closed the skating Rink down that night, and everyone was kicked out. The young man that got stomped had to get 43 staples in his head, and sustained broken ribs, but he would make a slow recovery. Rochelle and I were so traumatized that we drove back to the stoop and just sat in silence. Bryan and Ryan followed us back in their car. They got out of their car and started pouring drinks, and all the fellas out on the stoop recapped the events of the skating rink. This behavior was nothing unusual for the twins, this kind of thing went on all the time around the way and in the streets.

It was Easter weekend, and Ryan' s 5-year-old son was down from North Carolina on spring break. Ryan asked Rochelle and me to ride with him and Bryan to take Ryan Jr home. We were a little apprehensive, so Ryan threw in a shopping spree when we arrived. Rochelle gave me the eye, and then we agreed to go. Ryan had a few things to take care of before we left, so we met back up so we could start our excursion. I pulled up in my hooptie and parked it. Ryan pulled his old navy blue Thunderbird from the backyard and pulled onto the street. Ryan Jr was already strapped into the seatbelt in the back seat. Bryan, Rochelle, and I got in and we headed for the gas station. After Ryan filled up, we were off. On the highway, we went. The first two hours we all laughed and sang as we accelerated down the freeway. Ryan blessed us with his freestyle raps he made up and it was a party. After a few stops at different rest area, we were now entering North Carolina.

We stopped at Shoney's Restaurant to indulge in some southern cuisine. The buffet was irresistible. The creative way the fruit was displayed to entice the customers was amazing. The endless seafood hit the spot. Bryan cracked jokes on everyone that walked past our table. He was always a jokester. Ryan Jr played with his Jell-O while making truck sounds. We finished our meal and Bryan paid the bill. It was time to get back on the road and conquer our last 45 minutes. Ryan forced me to take the wheel and bring in the old Thunderbird for a landing. Rochelle and Bryan laughed the entire time I drove, as I struggled to see over the steering wheel. I was not used to driving big cars, so I had to put the driver's seat all the way up to reach the pedals. Through all their sarcasm, Ryan Jr remained sound asleep. On arrival, I precisely whipped into the driveway and parked, showing off my skills to all the passengers.

We all got out and stretched our legs. As we trailed up to the front door, Asia greeted us with such warmth and kindness and welcomed us in. Asia was Ryan Jr's mother. She was a pretty, and ambitious young lady. Asia was short and light skinned, with silky long jet black hair. Her eyes were very dark, with a slight Asian flare to them. I noticed immediately that Asia was about her business. She was a single parent, a homeowner at the age of 23, and drove a new silver 325I BMW. Asia and Ryan hooked up when they were 16. At the age 18, Asia became pregnant with Ryan Jr. When she graduated, she left the area and moved to North Carolina to escape the negative criticism. She attended Duke University and received a nursing degree and continued to strive for better.

Asia had put little Ryan in his bedroom and came back out to entertain us. We all hit it off well. For Rochelle and I meeting Asia for the first time, I would have to say she was cool. Asia had prepared food for us and a nice dessert to follow. She invited us all to the dining area to sip on a few grown-up cocktails and partake in grown-up conversation and laughs. After a couple of hours, it was late, and we were all exhausted. We thanked Asia for her wonderful hospitality and headed for the car to drive to our hotel.

Ryan went into the hotel and checked us in. He came back to the car and we grabbed our luggage. Bryan and Ryan entered their room, while Rochelle and I settled in next door. After taking our showers, we sat up and talked and eventually fell asleep.

It was Saturday morning, and Rochelle and I were awakened by the sound of the hotel telephone ringing. I answered the phone, and Bryan was speaking Spanish (so he thought), portraying to be a Hispanic housekeeper. After acting out his skit, he told us to get dressed so we could go to breakfast. Rochelle and I agreed to dress comfortably, so we threw on a cute sweat suit and a fresh sneaker. We went down to the car to meet the fellas, and Bryan had thrown it on. You would have thought we were going to a hip-hop music award or something. Bryan was known for his original style and was untouchable in the fashion game. He had on a green velour sweat suit with Gucci sneakers and matching Gucci hat. He topped it off with a large gold chain and gold Rolex Watch.

The four of us jumped in the car and headed to the local diner. The guys ordered a smorgasbord. I ordered French Toast with Maple Syrup and Turkey Bacon, while Rochelle ordered a Short Stack with Home Fries and a side of Pork Bacon. Good thing we all wore sweats, because our stomachs needed the extra room to sprawl out. We left the diner stuffed and silent. The next stop was the mall for our shopping spree. Ryan promised us ladies a shopping spree, and we sure enough were taking him up on his offer. We glided into the parking lot of the Crabtree Valley Mall. This mall was huge. The style in North Carolina was a tad bit slower than our style back home, but you could still find some cute items to rock back home. When we entered the mall, there was a beautiful fountain. The water sprouted out harmoniously. The elegant chandelier gave off a radiant illumination. We continued to walk, and that's when Bryan and Ryan both anxiously rushed over to a men's shoe store. This store had top of the line dress shoes for men. The brothers were in shoe heaven as they examined just about every shoe. I must say it was interesting. Some of these shoes were unique. One pair I felt was real crocodile and ostrich. The had the humps on the top of the shoe from the crocodile! It freaked me out. They were $650! The brothers resorted to getting 2 pairs of the same shoes each. They spent $1050 on 4 pairs of shoes. We left and caught the escalator upstairs to this upscale women's boutique. There clothes were classy and sexy. Right away, I was drawn to a black sheer dress on display. I paired it with a designer bag and matching pair of pumps. Rochelle picked out a black leather skirt with the black sheer top, and the matching pumps and hand bag. Ryan swiftly paid the bill with no problem, and we left the store.

We slowly walked toward the car and got in. Bryan volunteered to be the chauffer, while we all laid back and reclined as we headed to the hotel. We went to our rooms and took a little power nap. When I awoke, I figured I would beat Bryan to the punch. I called their room and spoke in a Jamaican accent and hung up on him. That's when Rochelle and I grabbed the deck of cards and went banging on the brothers' door. Ryan answered and let us in. We began to play spades and drink a few drinks. We ordered pizza and just had a fun night inside. When it got late, we left the fellas, and went back to our own room to unwind. Rochelle and I talked about the reason Ryan and I never hooked up. I explained to her we had more of a brother sister relationship than a romantic one. She understood and we gradually dozed off.

The next morning was Easter Sunday, and our weekend was coming to an end. It was time to check out and get on the road. We packed up the car and made way to the convenience store to fill up the gas tank. After that, toward the highway we went. The ride home was mellow.

I think everyone just wanted to sit back and take in their last sights and enjoy the ride while Bryn drove. Bryan put on the Sunday Oldies but Goodies, and we floated down the highway in the Thunderbird. We hit no traffic, so the ride home was rather short. Bryan and I switched drivers at the Maryland House Rest Stop, and I brought "Lady Bird" (The name we gave Ryan's car) on home. We were all exhausted when we finally got back, so we grabbed our bags and said our goodbyes. We each departed and went our separate ways to spend the remaining of the Easter holiday with our families. That trip was a memorable and much needed one.

THE WEDDING....
RECOGNIZE THE SIGNS

The aches and pains in my stomach, along with anxiety, awakened me. I had mixed emotions going on. I was excited and hesitant to get out of my bed. Dragging myself out of the bed and to my mirror to see if it's real. My head rushed with many thoughts of should I go through with it, or turn away. The phone calls poured in, asking, "Are you ready?" and "Are you ok?" My confirmation, it's my wedding day! After taking several deep breaths and talking to myself in the mirror, I decided I had to go through with this. I can't disappoint everyone who had been waiting on me. In less than 8 hours, I would walk down the aisle, my day had arrived.

Tyrell and I had known each other for over 10 years. He was my friend, Markus's little brother. Growing up, I never paid any attention to Tyrell, because he was younger than us. When Markus, and all our other friends would hang out, Tyrell could never come with us because of his age. Years later, Tyrell and I had stumbled upon one another at a job fair we both were attending for a new company that had recently opened. We were both hired, and worked for the same company, and that's when all the flirting began. Tyrell started work two hours after I did, so upon arrival, he would purposely walk down the main isle past my work area to get my attention. Tyrell would briefly stop and try to small talk with me while trying to slide in a slick comment or two. He had nice curly hair, so it seems as though he put a little extra activator in his hair when he thought he would see me. I still considered him "Markus's little brother", so I would just laugh at him and didn't take him seriously. Plus, at the time, I was in a relationship, so I just decided not to entertain his advances. Tyrell saw Carlise at the gym one day and inquired about me. She threw me under the bus and told him I was single. He then gave his number to Carlise to pass on to me. Carlise called me and told me about their conversation and how eager he was to take me out. She gave me his phone number, and I wrote it down. Tyrell had 2 small children, and

I had 3 teenagers from a previous relationship. I didn't like dating guys with younger kids, because not too far behind is baby mama drama. After a month of looking at the number, I finally called Tyrell. The initial conversation was dull. I could sense the hesitation and shyness in his voice. After a few more conversations, he began to build his confidence and got up enough nerve to ask me out on a date. His idea of a date was meeting him at his friend's house to watch a movie. As the months went by, we took things slowly and just gradually hooked up here and there. I wanted to use caution asI was just coming out of a long-term relationship. The more we talked, I noticed Tyrell was building a stronger relationship with God by consistently going to church, bible study, and reading his bible daily. That was a major plus, for Tyrell. Things between Tyrell and I grew, and eventually, we made it official that we were dating. Each morning, Tyrell would text me a scripture for the day, and we would discuss it later that evening. Things were good between us. I was reeled in by Tyrell's portrayal of putting God first in his life. We agreed to seal the deal and do things the right way in God's sight. It was time to tie the knot.

Guests traveled from great distances and spent great deals of money to partake in my special day. I couldn't turn back now. Again, my weakness kicking in, my weakness of pleasing everyone, except myself. I worried what others would say, and what they would think, while I suffered inside behind a decision I made to please everyone else. So now, the time had come to head to my salon to get prettied up for my big day. I walked in and all the ladies at the salon greeted me and gave me best wishes and words of wisdom. As the older women threw different questions out, the most important one remained unanswered, are you ready? My mouth said yes, but deep within my soul, the feeling I felt said otherwise. After styling my hair and applying my veil, my doubtful mindset changed and pulled it together. When I left the salon, it made me more confused than before I got there. I drove home looking at the things in nature I never took the time out to appreciate. The trees had a different meaning. The way they stood tall and strong made me view it as security and protection. When I looked upon the sky, its presence met the long stretch of puffy endless clouds. This gave me the feeling of love and gentleness. I imagined myself being wrapped in the clouds and taking a nice and peaceful nap.

When I reached the traffic light and stopped on red, I looked to my right and spotted hundreds of birds soaring in the air and moving fast. They had somewhere important to go. Observing this, I thought, follow your heart and break free now before it is too late. The second sign that made me rethink things showed itself. I got home and just wanted to relax and be alone to think and put things in perspective. I rejuvenated myself and, the time had arrived to start my journey to the hotel to get dressed. The 20-minute drive turned into 3 hours. Driving in complete silence the entire ride, I waited for a natural disaster, any emergency. Even the right comforting voice on the other end of a phone to rescue me...................but it never happened.

I arrived at the hotel and met with my childhood friend, LaTanya, whom had flown in from out of town to be with me on my big day. We sat and talked and figured out the right shades of blush and lipstick we needed. Next, we put on the formal attire. As I stepped into my gown and pulled it up, the butterflies resurfaced and took over my stomach. I glanced at the clock and continued to get dressed. My cell phone rang, and when I answered the phone, the reverend that would officiate the wedding told me she needed the paperwork from me to go ahead with the ceremony. She instructed me to go back home and get what she needed or the ceremony would not be official. I told her ok, and I hung up the phone. I took a moment to think to myself, should I bail out now? Is this a sign? After a few minutes, LaTanya volunteered to drive me back home to get what I needed.

After 15 minutes into our ride, my cellphone rang again. I answered the call, and it was Ryan! He called to wish me luck. We maintained a close friendship, despite his minor brush with the law. Ryan was in jail doing a 3-year bid for unknowingly receiving stolen property. The code of the street is not to snitch, so Ryan took his charge and rolled with it. He began to small talk and then he finally asked, are you sure you want to go through with this? I played it off and said, you're crazy; why did you ask me that? He said, "You and I are cool and I figured I call you to check on you, if you're not ready and you want to change your mind, you better tell me and I will send my boy to come get you." I wanted to yell from the top of my lungs, COME GET ME!!!!! Instead, I laughed it off and told him how crazy he was, and I had to go. My last lifeline had just been taken away. I felt sick.

I resumed the conversation with LaTanya and tried to act normally. When we arrived at my house, I went inside to get the paperwork and took one last look. It was my final view as a single woman. I hung my head and closed the door behind me and moped to the car. We headed back to the hotel, but by it being a Friday afternoon, traffic got heavy. The delays were persistent, but then we reached our destination. I gave the reverend the documents and went on to the hotel to finish up the last touches. The photographer took our pictures and, we headed off to the hall for the ceremony. On arrival, I was assigned my own private janitor's closet, because another wedding had run late. During my wait in the closet, employees kept coming in getting supplies and staring at me. One employee had the nerve to ask me if anyone knew I was in there. I said yes, I was placed here until they are ready for me. The employee said ok, left out, and closed the door. As I looked around, I stared at brooms, mops, and paper towels. After 20 minutes of waiting, the door swung open, and, the staff informed me they were ready.

As I walked down the aisle and peeked from underneath my veil, I screamed HELP! HELP! HELP! It was in my inner voice, so no one heard me. I put on a fake pageant smile to deceive everyone. As we exchanged vows, the rope around my neck tightened; time had run out. I took my last breath as a single woman and exhaled into marriage. When it came to I Do, and Kiss the bride, it was official. Officially the beginning of regrets.

THE MORNING AFTER

The next morning, I woke up hoping it was a big dream. That was not the case. When I looked in the mirror and saw the up do, curls, and day old make-up, I knew it was real. As we both got dressed and started our first day as one, it didn't go as planned. Tyrell and I had children from past relationships, and his child's mother left her phone home and could not be reached. With many attempts to contact her, we were unsuccessful. So, that meant a honeymoon was out the window, and we were babysitting for the weekend! This went in the books! This was the shenanigans of all shenanigans. I called Carlise, we met up, and I brought her up to speed on what was taking place. After a few hours, "the hubby" called and asked me to come back home. This was my first lesson of being submissive, I went.

When I got home, it was still "Three's Company", so nothing said was comprehended, and this was the start of my new life. I reflected on the signs shown the day before and just cried. The next few months were unbearable. After our union, he got hurt at work. This meant Tyrell was home every day being a pain. The medication he was taking contributed to the situation. The mood swings were out of this world. He was nice one minute and then the devil himself appeared. I recall one incident that occurred when I was up early one morning in the kitchen preparing dinner for the day. I had my headphones in, listening to my gospel music and just praising God while at the sink washing off vegetables.   He had entered the house with his son, and I didn't hear them. His son must have spoken to me, but by me wearing my headphones, I heard nothing. Suddenly, Tyrell ran up behind me and snatched me from behind and yelled in my face, saying, "I know you heard my son speak to you!" As I took off my headphones, I screamed back, "Don't you see me listening to music? How can I hear you if I have on headphones?" He became irate and aggressive and moved closer toward my face and cursed me out and disrespected me in front of his child.   My next move was defense, and I came out a raging bull.   Showing him he picked the wrong one to bully was the goal.

The priority was standing my ground, and I told him how silly he was for making a big scene over something so petty. He calmed to a certain degree, only because his son was there. That blew over, and the next month or two were good. I thought things between us were getting better. The financial situation got better, because the disability checks came regularly, A lot of stresses was lifted, and, we continued to go to church to get guidance and the spiritual connection we needed from God. It wasn't long, before the devil came back in to carry on with his plan.

LaTanya's sister had passed away, and it was the day of the funeral.   I had to be there to show support and strength. I attended the funeral and left for a few to go back home and change. My plan was to go back to spend time with LaTanya's family. I went home to do a few odds and ends and change my clothes. When I got in the door, I went straight to the kitchen to whip up a quick meal. After doing the dishes and straightening up the kitchen, I headed for the bedroom to look in my closet and find something comfortable to wear. I pulled my jeans off the plastic hanger and slid into them. Next, I stepped into my tall suede brown boots. I bent to lace my boots, and as I was finished and stood up straight in walks the devil himself. I stood in the walk -in closet in my bra, jeans and boots, and the questions begin.

Tyrell had asked me where I was going in an angry voice. I responded, "Back to spend time with my friend and her family at the repass before they head back home." He yelled, "You think you're slick, you got to get all dressed up to go visit your friend?" I said, "I want to look present-able! I haven't seen LaTanya's family in years!" He still insisted I was up to something. Suddenly, he took the cup of water he was drinking and threw it in my face and all over my hair to sabotage me from going back. We fussed and fought. I felt disrespected and violated. I got my keys and bolted for the door. When I got in my car, I locked my doors and sat in my whirlwind of emotions to pull it together. I called LaTanya to let her know I was on my way back to spend time with her. She said, "Girl, we left, we're on the turnpike headed back home!" My heart fell to my feet!

My end of the phone was silent! I had to live with the fact I disappointed my friend! Not being there for her when she needed me the most was unacceptable. I apologized to her, but, she assured me things were ok. When we hung up, I cried the ugliest cry ever! My world was so dark with everything I had been secretly battling. I drove to the river and just sat on the bench to watch the waves crash back and forth against the strong rocks. It had started to drizzle, but I didn't care. I just needed to feel peace in my soul and regain my self-worth. I formulated a strategy to reclaim my self-respect and dignity. I refused to allow anyone else to dictate my life. I got back in my car and put on my Gospel CD and allowed the music to minister to my spirit. When I arrived home, he was asleep so I proceeded with caution. I undressed and got into bed and prayed to God for a better tomorrow.

SURPRISE SURPRISE

I recall leaving for work early one day to start my long commute. I got to work earl, so I sat in my car and just meditated. While still in my car, my phone rang so I answered it. On the other end was Carlise. We talked and caught up on the latest gossip and reminisced on old memories. I noticed Carlise voice had changed and she said, "I want to tell you something, but I don't know how to tell you!" I said, "Go ahead and tell me, what's going on?" She said, "Don't tell him I told you, but, Tyrell is cheating on you!" I said "Huh?" She went into detail about how long the affair had been going on and the mistress's name.

I became dumbfounded! Anxiety took over my body, and the air in my body escaped. I started my car and anxiously left the parking lot and headed for the highway. As I drove and gathered my thoughts, I checked out a few things on my own. I drove past the mistress's house and her car was in the driveway. She belonged to a family of her own, so I guess this was a pastime thing between the two of them. The thought of knocking on her door and exposing everything crossed my mind, but because of the innocent children and her boyfriend, I played it cool. I went on home and sat on this information for a few weeks. This secret ate at my core. I did my best to stay normal. There were repeated thoughts of dousing him with gasoline while he slept and lighting a match, but again, I thought of the innocent children at hand. It finally made sense why he had the mood swings and insecurities. He didn't want me to find out, so that's why he had to keep tabs on me. He could not juggle the two situations he had going on. I continued to do my daily routine to keep a form of normalcy.

I went to work as scheduled and put my headset on to listen to calming music. My first break, I sat in the break room and chatted with co-workers and laughed. Break ended, and I went back to work, and continued to listen to my music. After 30 minutes of smooth grooves, a blocked id call came across my phone. I normally don't answer strange numbers nor blocked id numbers, but my gut instructed me to answer the call with so much drama in the air. I slid the answer button to the right to connect the call, and the voice on the other end jolted my heart. The feeling of being shocked with an AED (automated external defibrillator) monitor is what I felt. The well-mannered voice on the other end asked for me and identified himself as the one and only Satin, the mistress's boyfriend. I could not believe the other piece of the puzzle contacted me.

We talked for hours and compared notes about each of our significant other's activities. I was greatly surprised by the pleasantness in his voice, considering the circumstances. We talked from 12:30 a.m. until 6:00 a.m., the length of my shift. We both agreed to get off the phone after a long first conversation. Satin ended the call by saying, "I apologize for having to contact you under this difficult situation, but I want to say best wishes to you in the future." I said, "Thank you" and hung up. The entire ride home, I played the conversation in my head. This remained a secret I kept to myself until I figured out my next move. I got home, showered, and jumped in bed. I tossed and turned, still reviewing the conversation from the previous hours. Finally, I dozed off, leaving the cares of the world behind......temporarily.

I woke up that afternoon with time slipping away fast. I sat home alone, enjoying my stress-free environment and loved every minute. I started cooking dinner as I waited for the children to get home from school. Suddenly, my cell phone rang, and when I looked, blocked id appeared. I panicked. There went the 4th ring from the incoming call. I hesitated to answer, but I did. I said, "hello". Sure, enough, on the other end, the one and only Satin. He said, "I hope I am not disturbing you. Can you talk?" I said "Yes", go ahea, what's up?" Satin wanted to get clarity on things we discussed, and after 15 minutes, we hung up. I got things in place on the home front, and before you knew it, 6p.m. had arrived, time to make the donuts. My mind still tried to grasp everything that transpired. With my world spiraling around me, I needed to get a clear picture of what exactly was going on.

I took my first break and came back to start work. My phone rang. I looked at the clock on the wall, and it read 12:30 a.m. When I looked at my phone, it was blocked id! I thought, no it can't be. My next thought was, ok now, what else do we need to say? Again, I answered and the suave voice on the other end of the receiver was Satin. We talked about the unfortunate situation going on, but I noticed the conversation changed and went into another direction. We discussed our hobbies, likes and dislikes, places we traveled, and hit it off. It felt awkward, but it was another break of dawn conversation.

Each day, I received good morning texts, and phone calls more frequently. I found myself waiting on these calls and text messages to put a smile on my face. Like a drug addict chasing a hit, our conversations were my high to take me away from the pain in my life. This continued for a month. I could sense we both were looking forward to the intellectual conversing more and more.

I made up my mind to put the cards on the table. When Tyrell came in from work, I told him we needed to talk. I confronted him about the affair, and he denied it. I said "Well if this is a lie, let's both go and meet with her and her boyfriend to solve the problem." He refused! I told him, if this marriage means something to you, you will prove nothing is going on…. he still refused to confront the issue. I left it alone, but at that point, I had the answer to my question…it was true.

THE LAST STRAW

Three months had gone by and still no resolution to the problem at hand. I tried to hang on and make things work between us. I tried to get things back on track and plan an evening out, so I bought tickets to a famous stage play that came to town for a few days. The night of the show, I was soaking my aching body in the tub, when I heard a knock on the bathroom door. Before I responded, Tyrell came in and handed me the telephone and left. I said hello, and to my surprise, it was Ryan. He was checking up on me to see how the new married life was going. In an around about way, in code, I hinted to Ryan that things weren't too good. Ryan again, being my protector, said, "He ain't putting his hands on you or anything, is he?" I played it off and said, "He ain't crazy". Ryan and I laughed and talked a little more and then the operator joined the conversation to let us know Ryan had 1 minute left and then the phone would disconnect. We said our goodbyes and disconnected the call.

To my surprise, Tyrell's insecurities kicked in, once again. He was at the bathroom door eavesdropping the whole time. He didn't like that Ryan and I were close, so he busted in the door and attacked me while I was still in the tub. I fought him off long enough to get out of the tub and grab a towel and run out into our bedroom. As I frantically looked for clothes to get dressed and make my escape, he stood by the ironing board, ironing his shirt. While ironing, he yelled at me, trying to mimic me about how I was laughing and giggling on the phone with Ryan. I told him he was crazy and delusional, and that's when he snapped. He charged at me with the hot iron in his one hand and chocked me with the other hand. He put the scorching iron close to my face and threaten me. I calmed down, because I didn't want to take him up on his offer to defuse the situation. I refused to go to the show with him, but he forced me to go.

Due to the altercation, we arrived at the play at the halfway intermission. Inside, I felt like the scene from

"What's love got to do with it", when Tina and Ike had just fought but had to play it off and perform anyway. While we were at the play, I kept telling myself, this is it! I planned my steps of leaving, because the next incident would put one of us in an early grave and the other a life sentence. As I looked around the room at all the other couples, I wondered who else was going through what I was going through. All dressed up and looking pretty on the outside, but dark and full of pain on the inside. I thought of standing up in the middle of the theater and yelling "Please help me." I squirmed and twisted in my seat the entire time. I didn't want his arm around me, nor did I want to feel his body rubbing against mine in those tight theater seats. The irony is the play was about marriage and staying together, but for me, I had nothing left to give. When the play dismissed, I hurriedly walked down the steps and toward the front door. The crowd was taking pictures with the cast members of the play, so I got stuck there. Tyrell caught up with me, and we exited the door together. The walk to the parking garage was grueling! In heels, we had to walk a good 6 blocks. I walked on one side of the street, while Tyrell walked on the other. We finally made it to the parking garage, and the attendant retrieved the car. When they pulled up, I got in the passenger side, locked my seat-belt, and stared out the window the entire ride.

We rode in silence from the play home. No apology or anything came from Tyrell's lips. We entered the home, and I undressed and got in the bed. I stared at the ceiling all night waiting for daybreak to escape. I woke up around 7am and got showered and dressed. I contemplated how I would get out of the house. I lied and said I would go get breakfast for us and asked Tyrell what he wanted. He gave me his request, and then I grabbed my keys and took one last look around. At that point, I knew it would be the last time I would be held captive behind these walls.

I walked out the front door and got into my car, put my seatbelt on, and drove away. I decided I was not coming back and left for good. I left all my material possessions behind. I didn't care about starting over and buying new things. I needed to leave that toxic relationship. Who would have thought 7 months into our union, it would be over! Again, I worried about what people would say?

BONNIE AND CLYDE
TIME OF MY LIFE

As I put the pieces of my life back together, the phone calls from Satin came in regularly. We had been communicating for 3 months. Since I was separated and the divorce was being processed, Satin and I agreed it was time to put a face with these mysterious voices we both had been hearing for months. The anticipation was growing heavy, leading up to when we would meet. On that day, I got dressed and applied my make-up. Then, I smoothed out my lip gloss. To stay calm, I talked to myself on the ride to meet him. Next, I called Carlise to explain where I was going, and who I was meeting, in case I ended up missing.

When I reached our meeting place, I got out of the car and walked up to the door and knocked. The door swung open, but no one was in the doorway. He showed his sense of humor from the start, because he was hiding behind the door. I entered and looked around. As the door closed, I saw a silhouette of a well-sculpted body. The silhouette moved toward me and came to life. I observed the tattoo art on his arms and neck, and the shine of his freshly shaved bald head. The slight slant of his eyes made him mysterious. The curiosity drew me in. When he finally spoke, it was a match from the phone conversations, and I said yes, that's him. We were both shy at first, so we stared at one another. We entertained one another's company for an hour, and then I decided to leave. As I stood up to go, he walked toward me and laughed and joked about how short I was. He then pulled me into his chiseled chest and held me tight. I laid my head on his fresh, white shirt and treasured the moment. After 30 seconds, I lifted my head off his chest to turn and leave, and that's when Satin seductively kissed me. I could smell the aroma of Blistex projecting from his lips, which were so soft I wanted to bite them. He walked me to the door, and we agreed to talk later.

I stepped quickly to my car to call Carlise to let her know everything was ok. She could hear the excitement in my voice, which made her excited. She said "So, how did he look?" I replied, "Girl, he was fine!" She busted out laughing, and I explained to her play- by -play what happened. We ended the call, and I went to my temporary residence to rest and just think things over. While laying across the bed, my phone rang with blocked id rolling across the screen. I smiled and answered. Satin said, "I don't want you to take this the wrong way, but I didn't want you to leave." I laughed and said, "Aww" He told me how beautiful I was and how my voice matched my appearance. I came out and told him I thought he was handsome too. He then automatically made plans for us for later that night, so I guess he was interested. Later that night, we went out to dinner and had a few cocktails. We discussed past relationships and our goals. We both agreed life was short and the goal towards happiness is living life to the fullest. From that day, each day, we were doing a different excursion. Going to the movies, attending jazz concerts, and sampling different restaurants throughout the east coast. My birthday was approaching, and I wanted it to be a blast! Satin told me to pick wherever I wanted to go, and we were going. I thought on it for a few days and reached different places and made my decision. I was set to go to Baltimore to the Inner Harbor for my birthday.

The day we were set to leave, everything went wrong. We left later than we had planned, so traffic was bumper to bumper. I was upset and insisted we turn around and go back. Satin said, "No, this is your birthday weekend. This is where you wanted to go, and I want your birthday to be special, so we are going!" I sighed and tried to stay calm. Traffic let up, and it was smooth sailing! The highway was ours. As we zoomed down the highway, the breeze from the night air soothed me.

After arriving in Baltimore, it was as if the rest of the world was on pause. We walked around and took in the sights. The lights dazzled, the waves from the harbor crashed against the dock. The air was cool and crisp. We had scheduled to take the dinner cruise that evening. Satin and I took our pictures before boarding the cruise to capture my birthday memory. We quickly made friends with other couples on the ship. To our surprise, that night was a private event, and all the people looked very spiffy. The girls had on beautiful stylish gowns. The gentlemen were well-groomed in their tuxedos. Watching these people set the mood for the party.

The ship took off, and I felt all my worries being left at the dock as we set sail. We engaged in some intellectual conversation, laughed, and sipped on a few Apple Martinis. The DJ played a good beat that made everyone run for the dance floor. We began to dance and party and enjoy the ride. When we finished dancing, we took a stroll out on the outside deck. The chill in the air felt great and gave off the feeling of tranquility. We were going through a lot, but none of that mattered at the moment, nor did it exist. Gazing at the ripples of the waves, and the stars dancing in the sky, made it a memorable evening. As the sail came to an end, we looked around as if to say our last goodbyes. The ship disembarked, so we took a walk around the harbor. It started out cool, but I couldn't play it off any longer. I had to let it be known my feet were hurting. Satin laughed and took my hand, slowed his stride, and turned me around to head back to the car.

As he opened my car door, I gently slid into the leather seats and kicked off my shoes. He got in, started the engine, and cranked up the heat to get the chill off our hands and feet. We maneuvered out of the parking lot and headed for the hotel. After this long day, it was time to relax. I opened the door to our room, and there were balloons, a beautiful strawberry shortcake, and a bottle of Dom Perignon. I was impressed. I could not stop smiling. I was thinking wow, we are just getting to know each other, and he put this much thought into my birthday. I thanked him and took off my shoes and removed my jacket. I walked to the bathroom to run the water to the Jacuzzi. I opened the bathroom door, and hanging on a soft satin hanger was a gorgeous black lace Cami Top with matching black satin pants. My smile was everlasting. I returned from the bathroom and gave Satin the most grateful hug and peck on his smooth lips. I thanked him again for such a memorable birthday. He said, "Like I told you, I wanted to make sure your birthday was special." I went back into the bathroom and enjoyed my bubble bath. I played my playlist from my phone and just laid back and took it all in. I sang to Beyonce's song, entitled *Party*. I was in my zone, and it was all about me. I got out of the tub, and applied my lotion and my smell goods. I gently took the lingerie off the hanger. As I pulled the lace top over my head, I felt more mature and sophisticated. I easily stepped into the satin pajama pants and pulled them up. Immediately, I was a new woman. I opened the door to the bathroom and walked out into the sitting area in the hotel room. From a slight crack in the curtain, I saw Satin outside on the balcony. I slid the glass door and went outside to join him, and he was in awe. His piercing eyes moved down my body from head to toe. Satin said, "You really look beautiful." I think I did a good job picking that out." I agreed. He then said, "I wanted to get you something nice, but not too revealing." I didn't want you to be uncomfortable, nor did I want to overstep my boundaries."

I sat down at the patio table on the balcony and Satin poured the Dom! We tossed to our friendship, becoming closer, and my birthday all in one. We admired the night sky and the weird lights from the many planes passing by. The breeze was breath takin, but, it got chilly. We went inside to get warm. The Dom made me tired, so I kept yawning. Satin said, "Ok, let's call it a night. I see you can't hang." I got in the bed and pulled up the blanket. Satin said, "I want to show you that I am a gentleman." He took the extra blanket out of the closet and opened the pull-out couch and made up his bed for the night. Before he got in, he came over to me and kissed me on the forehead and said, "Sweet Dreams." I said goodnight, and he walked back over to his pad for the night, and before I knew it, I heard snoring. He was out like a light. This was a birthday to remember.

PINK RIBBON

My mother was always a quiet and easygoing person. She was always a stay at home mom and was content with being a wife and mother. While my father's health changed, my mother was right by his side every step of the way. While making sure my father was ok, my mother noticed changes within her own body she kept to herself. She put herself on the back burner and gave her undivided attention to her husband. As time went on, my mother finally went to the doctors and explained to them what she was experiencing.

They ran tests and sent out for the results. A few days later, the doctor's office called to tell my mother to come back.

At the doctor's visit, the doctor informed my mother she had stage 3 breast cancer, and at once, they needed to do a mastectomy. That moment our lives changed. My mother came home and told us what was going on and told us not to worry. She had placed it in God's hands, so she wasn't worried. Her surgery was scheduled for the following week. We made the proper provisions to be there the day of the surgery. It was a lot of emotion leading up to the day of surgery. We suggested she get a second opinion and even try holistic methods. My mother's mind was made up to go through with the procedure.

The day of surgery, we had overwhelming support. My Aunt Barb and Uncle Butch from Virginia, and my cousin Joe from Indiana. It was a great feeling to see the family stand strong and come together. It was time to start prepping my mother for surgery, so we had to pair up into twos to say our farewells until after surgery. I waited until last and entered the room. My mother grabbed my hand tight and squeezed it. I knew that was the first sign of fear, but she remained strong. She gave me her wedding band to hold onto until the surgery was finished. I felt the power in that ring and the years of dedication of the marriage between my mother and father. I gave my mom a hug and kiss and told her I would see her after surgery. I turned around and left the room, so my mother couldn't see my tears. I had to be strong for everyone there. My dad called from home, because his health was not that good, but he wanted to show his love. The nurse came to wheel my mom away and to make sure she was in good hands. We went to eat and socialize. Three hours later, the doctor appeared and called us in the conference room. She explained the entire procedure and told us everything went well, and she wanted to know if we had questions. In the recovery room, my mother was still groggy, so we let her rest. She stayed in the hospital for a few days, and then she was released.

When my mother came home, we had to drain her incision and measure how much fluid was being released each day. My mother had to arm exercises to prevent stiffness in her arm. We pitched in and did the household duties, while my mother got better. It wasn't long until she was back to normal and wanted no help. The next phase for my mother was the chemotherapy. She had treatments 3 times a week for 4 months. As time went on, we began to see the changes in her. She experienced hair loss, weight loss, and changing in her skin complexion. Some days she was fine, others she was nauseated and would vomit. My mother decided not to let this disease win. She had two things on her side to help her conquer cancer. The first was God, and the second was her sister-in-law (my aunt), the one and only Rev. Susie Mae Johnson. Between the two, you would get the beating of your life, so cancer had to disappear. My mother had to do a few sessions of radiation to make sure the cancer was gone. When this was over, I looked at my mother and said, "She is a fighter!"

The courage and strength my mother carried the entire time was phenomenal. Not once did she complain, nor did she ever question God. Observing my mother's journey down the road of recovery was hard, but it gave me the motivation to conquer anything that came my way.

FOREVER CHANGED

My morning started as any other typical morning, fighting the rush hour traffic like I did daily. I arrived at work and began to go into the zone. It was the beginning of December, so I put on my Christmas music and listened to get into the Christmas spirit. As the work day got into full swing, it was a little hectic. By lunch time, I told myself I was going straight home to relax. About 30 minutes before the end of my shift, my mother called to see if I would stop by the hospital to see my dad after work. I explained to her I was exhausted and dirty and I would visit him the next day. She said ok, and we hung up. When I clocked out from work and got in my car, I found a soothing jazz station for the ride home. I planned on putting up the Christmas Tree when the children got home from school and decorate for the holiday season. I got home, ran my bathwater, and thought about nothing else but relaxing. I created my own oasis, dimmed the bathroom lights, poured a glass of wine, played soft music, and I was in ecstasy. My mother called me to tell me they were back from the hospital and to tell me how the visit with my dad went. She told me my dad was playing and joking with my son, and he would be home in a few days. I reiterated I would visit him tomorrow. We hung up. and I continued with my bath. The children entered from a long day of school, so that was the end of my spa day. I got out and made a quick dinner for the children, and we all settled down for the evening. Next, I laid down and watched T.V. and dozed off. Awakened by the sound of my phone ringing, I grabbed the phone, and my mother's number was displayed on the caller id.

I answered, and I heard my mother struggling to get her words out.

I never heard her sound like this before. I jumped up and said "What mom, what?" She burst out crying and said the nurse from the hospital just called and my dad's heart stopped! They were trying to resuscitate him now, but we must get there. I told her I was on my way. I threw on my clothes and got the kids ready and headed to the car. They kept asking what was going as we drove to the hospital, and I had to release it. I said, pop pop's heart stopped, so they are trying to restart it, so we must get there quickly.

The entire car was in chaos. My daughters screamed and cried. My son called me from my mother's house pleading for me to hurry. Hearing the pain in his voice and the way he cried, I floored it. I busted in the hospital parking lot, and I recognized my brother Douglas's car. He and my sister-in-law were standing by the car. I flew into a nearby parking spot, and we all jumped out. The hospital automatic doors opened, and my brother was coming out, crying. I said, "What's going on?" He hung his head and hugged me and said, "He's gone!" I wanted to lay down in the parking lot and get run over by a cement truck. I had to pull myself together, because my children were in distress. We all entered the hospital room, and I was still in disbelief. It can't be! It's got to be a mistake! When more family members arrived, the realization settled in. When my aunt Rev Susie Mae walked in, I knew it was no longer a dream. After hours of grieving, it was time for us to go.

The ride home, I looked high to the sky to see if I would get a sign my dad was with the Lord. I don't recall seeing anything unusual, but holding on to the peaceful and calm look on my father's face when I left his bedside, I knew he was in God's kingdom. The days leading to the funeral were long and grueling. I had to be strong for my mother and my children.

The day of the funeral, my sister, Ann, called to check in to let us know she was in route and would be there soon. We all kept checking our phone, as the time for the funeral was getting near. The family car pulled up to get us and still nothing from Ann. We arrived at the church and were rapidly escorted in. We sat down and looked around, and still no sign of Ann. Every time the door opened, I looked back to see if it was her, it wasn't. The funeral was over, and we were all leaving the cemetery. We checked our phones again for missed calls, but there were none from her. The family conducted the repass, and everyone disbursed after a few hours. The immediate family went back to my mom's house to clean up and talk. We all discussed how Ann didn't show up for the funeral. When you thought it couldn't get any worse, the phone rang to my mother's house. She answered and, it was the same hospital that called about my dad. This time, they were calling to inform us that Ann was accidentally struck by a car trying to cross the street. She had head trauma, bleeding on the brain, broken facial bones, a broken pelvis, and needed help to breath. They also gave her a 30% survival rate. We just buried my father, now traveling back to the same hospital to face the crisis with my sister.

Lord, please give us strength! We can't do this without you, Lord! On arrival, it was a sad sight. The ICU was quiet and cold. It was a depressing feeling that had overcome me. As I pulled the curtain back to see Ann, it was hard to recognize her with all the swelling. The doctor explained the next few days would be crucial. They needed to see how bad her brain was. The driver of the automobile was a middle-aged Caucasian male. He was a prominent member of his community and sat on the city council board. He admitted to having a few drinks right before the accident. The officer at the scene even gave a statement that, when he arrived at the scene, he smelled alcohol on the councilman. After forensic testing, the councilman results came back under the legal limit. Of course, they did! Therefore, he wouldn't be charged with D.U.I. As the legal aspect played out, Ann still fought to get better. Every time we asked questions or demanded info pertaining to the case, we were given the run around. It was now Christmas Day, and it was a Christmas like no other. None of us had the Christmas spirit. We were all still numb from the double whammy to our family. I didn't even put up a tree that year. I saw the growth in my children that year because they didn't even ask for anything. They wanted their pop-pop back, and that was all. My children went to my mother's house on Christmas Day to keep her company. I stayed home and curled up in my bed and cried all day. That day was Christmas, which made the pain hurt even more. It's funny how you can have 20 friends and still feel alone. This was my darkest day. I understood how people became depressed around the holidays and acted irrationally. Myself included, we play things off in public so well that no one knows what you are going through. The days that followed, I tried to get out of my rut. I didn't want to get dressed. I didn't want to go to work. I shut down.

After 2 1/2years, the case was winding down. In one week, Ann had her first court appearance for her lawsuit. Ann, my mother, and I met up with Ann's attorney in the hallway of the courthouse. Her attorney seemed timid and obedient. Her name was Ms. Wilson. She was a new attorney fresh out of school, so there was a lack of experience. She was young with a reddish bob hairstyle, and red eyeglasses. Her perfume smelled horrible, like something your grandma would get you from the dollar store. She went through everything with Ann in the hall to prepare her for the court hearing. We entered the court room, and it was a private hearing, with only about 10 people total, including the judge. The judge started the hearing and to paint a picture of Ann, the other attorney dug into Ann's past. Her run-ins with the law as a juvenile came back to be used against her. The court tried to portray Ann as a troubled black woman with issues. Councilman Reed, the one who struck Ann, was glorified for the good work he did in the community. To dress things up, they disclosed his educational degrees and awards. After 2 hours of testimony, court was adjourned. We had to meet back at 1pm to hear the verdict.

At 1pm, court was back in session. The judge recapped all the findings to reach his verdict. The judge ruled in favor of Councilman Reed and said Ann was negligent crossing the street. Ann would not be compensated for any of her injuries.

Ms. Wilson looked confused. Ann hung her head low with disgust. The gut wrenching jolt I felt was painful. As we all exited the court room, my mother was silent. As Ann and I discussed the unjust ruling, my mother finally intervened. She said,

"It's finally done and over with it. It could have been worse. You could have died, but God kept you here for a reason, so let it go." Even though we wanted justice, mom was right. Ms. Wilson caught up to us and apologized. She hugged Ann and walked off teary-eyed. It was a long process, but to God be the glory. Ann pulled through, but it took several years of recovery. She lost some of her memory, which may be a good thing not having to relive her experience, but for me, I would be forever changed.

TAKE ME AWAY

With the beating that my family and I had just taken, Satin thought it would be a good idea to get away. He told me he missed the old fun and playful "A" and needed her back. Satin had planned a very overdue vacation for the two of us. It was Fourth of July weekend, and it was time to break free. We flew from Philadelphia to Ft Lauderdale just to cool out for a few days. Our hotel had an incredible view. We could look out over the pool at the amazing Tiki Bar. The native Palm Trees that swayed from the breeze gave off a paradise atmosphere.

Satin and I got settled in and went downstairs to the hotel restaurant. They had a succulent Prime Rib dinner special going on, so I tried it. It was to die for. Satin ordered the tangy and rich Crab Imperial. When dinner was over, we walked outside to the Tiki Bar. There, I ordered a Mai Tai and Satin ordered a beer. We sat and enjoyed the music and watched children horseplay in the pool. A couple came and sat cross from us, and we talked about things like where we all were from, and politics. The couple were from New Zealand. The wife's accent was so proper and crisp. I enjoyed hearing her speak. After the nice couple left, we headed up to our hotel and observed the scenery from above. As we gazed outside for about 5 minutes, out of nowhere, there were beautiful fireworks. The vibrant colors shot up in the atmosphere. The choreography of the fireworks was unbelievable. I remember a white and purple display that went up and then paused in the air. Then it released the sparkler affect. It was awesome. The colors gave off a peaceful vibe. The display went on for about 40 minutes, until midnight. When the show concluded, you could hear the other people that had been watching the show cheering and whistling. A short while after the show, I felt the tropical drinks, and I felt tired. I laid across the bed and immediately fell asleep. The next thing I knew Satin, was waking me up at 7:32 a.m. The restaurant downstairs only served dinner, so we had to go out for breakfast. There was a Dunkin Donuts down the block, so we took an early morning stroll before Florida's humidity came over us. That early in the morning, the temperature was already 80 degrees. When we got to Dunkin Donuts, I ordered 2 glazed donuts and a medium orange juice. Satin ordered an ice coffee and an egg and cheese sandwich on a croissant. We paid for our food, and went out the door. On our way back, there were 3 homeless men standing along the sidewalk asking passersby for things. The men looked sweaty and disheveled. Satin switched places with me and got on the right side of me. He then walked over to the three men and gave each an undisclosed amount of money. They thanked him, and were greatly appreciative. As we walked away, Satin said, "When I see the homeless, I always try to stop and help give what I can." You never know if it's an angel in disguise." I agreed because I was also taught that. We made it back to the hotel and ate. We relaxed for a few hours, and Satin said, "Come on, we got to pack." I said, "Yeah right, whatever. We came all the way down here to stay one day?" He said, "Can you just do what I asked you to do, please?" I got my things together, and we called for a taxi.

The taxi came and drove us to our next destination. As we turned onto a long road, I saw hundreds of yellow cabs parked. Then I noticed an abundance of Palm Trees. When a break between the trees became available, I could see water. Next, the taxi drove around the curve, and there before our eyes were two gigantic cruise ships. That's right, Satin had booked us a cruise to the Bahamas! I was surprised, but Satin had never been out of the United States, so he was ecstatic. This was his first major vacation. We got out of the taxi, and joined the other passengers in line. Finally, it was our turn to check in and clear security. After that process, we went upstairs to get our cabin information and set up our account. At the next station, we had to choose our dinner time for the remainder of the trip. Once that was over, we proceeded to the vessel. Satin's eyes were big. He looked around in amazement, taking in everything. All the passengers were aboard, and the captain made his announcements. Then the captain sounded his horn for takeoff. Our cruise had officially started. The dj on the upper level of the deck played all the latest hits to get the passengers hyped. Satin and I walked around the ship to make ourselves familiar with where all the hot spots were. We located a casino, comedy club, and a movie theater. We stopped at the buffet and grabbed a bite to eat, and then headed outside to sit on the deck. Satin and I relaxed in the lounge chairs and admired the view. We snapped pictures and played around. Then we went back to the cabin and got some rest.

When we woke up, we got dressed and headed out for the nightlife. We found a karaoke lounge that caught our attention. We found a table and got comfortable. There was a younger Caucasian woman that took the stage. When she got on the mic to sing, she captured everyone's attention in the lounge. She sang Whitney Houston's *I Will Always Love You*. The purity in her voice was natural. She possessed such grace and poise. If you closed your eyes, you would think it was Whitney herself. When she finished, the lounge gave her a standing ovation. She was great. We listened to a few more performances, and then we left. We called it a night, so we could be up and ready in the morning for when we docked at the Bahamas.

It was 8 a.m. and it was time to disembark. I wanted to look native, so I put on my purple, white, and black dashiki dress with my black gladiator sandals. The islanders were waiting for the vacationers to step off the ship to begin their hustle. They tried to sell t-shirts, jewelry, and other souvenirs. Some islanders offered discount taxi rides to make money. The cruise line had already warned us they weren't licensed taxi driver, so it was unsafe to use them. The Bahamian women also offered hair braiding to the ladies that passed. Satin and I entered our shuttle and headed down to the Grand Bahama Beach. On arrival, the water looked fake. It was so blue and refreshing that it reminded me of the blue-sky soda I liked drinking when I was a kid. We got all set up on the beach and took advantage of the luxurious water. We swam and played in the water, while watching parasailing and kayaking.

Next, we washed off and set out to see the town. We found a simple little restaurant, called After Deck Bar and Grill, to try native cuisine. Satin ordered a Chicken Cesar Salad and a lemon water, because it was so hot outside. I ordered the Jerk Shrimp over white rice and a Bahama Mama. The food was all right. I expected it to be a little more native. When we were about to leave, out of nowhere came an older Bahamian gentleman dressed in full native costume. He wore an oversized white, orange, and green feathery head dress. He also had the feathery poncho to match. He told us about the history of the island. It was informative. Then we left and continued walking around the town. We stopped in a gift shop that sold cigars and liquor. Satin decided to live a little and purchase a Cuban Cigar (don't know if it was real or not). When we left there, we went back down to the beach and relaxed. We took some more pictures for our memories and picked up our backpacks to leave. Suddenly, Satin said, "Wait a min-ute." He opened his backpack and pulled out a plastic bag and put sand from the Bahama beach in it. He wanted to take a part of paradise with him. He sealed the bag, put it in his back pack, and we left to head to the shuttle.

The shuttle arrived and several of us jumped aboard. It was hot on the shuttle and everyone fanned themselves. Passengers complained. It felt like the air conditioner was blowing out hot air. The driver ignored all the complaints and pulled off slowly. We arrived back at the ship and quickly got off the shuttle. We had to go through cus-toms again to board the ship. After we passed through, we went back to the cabin to shower and rest. Satin and I planned to have a very special night. We woke up at 5p.m. to prepare for our 6p.m. reservation. This was the night we planned to do it big. I touched up my make-up and put on my lip gloss. I stepped into my white sundress with the rhinestones on the shoulders. I put on my glass pumps with the rhinestones to match. When I stood up, Satin came up behind me and placed a beautiful rhinestone necklace shaped like a necktie. His taste was so on point that the necklace laid perfectly between my cleavage. Satin put on his white linen pants and matching shirt. He finished by squirting his cologne as we headed out the door. When we got off the elevator, there was a photographer taking pictures. He stopped Satin and me and wanted to try some new backgrounds on us, because he liked our coordination with our attire. We gave in, and the photographer told us to come back after dinner.

When we entered the dining ballroom all eyes were on us. You would have thought we were celebrities or something. The hostess took us to our table, and we were seated. We had stuffed flounder for dinner and double chocolate cake for dessert. We left dinner, and went back to check on our pictures. By the time we arrived, the photo store was closing soon. The guy laid out our photos, so we could choose what we liked. Because they were about to close, we got a $300 photo package for $60! We took the photos to our cabin. We changed our clothes, and put on some comfortable clothes to have fun. Our next stop was to check out the outdoor club. We got there, and it was breathtaking. The breeze softly moved through the deck. This night was glow night, so as guests entered, they were giving out glow necklaces and strobes. It was awesome! We looked around to get a feel of the vibe, and then we found a table to sit. We ordered two Long Island's and got up and walked to the side of the ship. Satin reached into his pocket and pulled out his Cuban Cigar and lit it. After he inhaled, there followed several coughs. I laughed. After smoking half, he put it out because he couldn't handle it.

We returned to our seats and grooved to the music. On the left was a hot tub with three younger females in it. They were talking and having fun. Then, out of nowhere, a young flamboyant guy came along and danced on the side of the hot tub. He was annoying and persistent. He hopped up on the side of the hot tub and started twerking! At this point, the ladies got out. After Satin and I observed the guy's erratic behavior, we moved our seating to stay clear of the drama. As Satin and I began having a deep conversation, the guy started dancing wild all around from table to table. When he got to our table, he pulled me by hand for me to get up and dance with him. Quickly, Satin grabbed his arm and pushed it away. The guy and Satin exchanged words, and the next thing I know, Satin stood up and punched the guy in the face. He was a thin guy, so he went falling backwards into the hot tub. He gracefully got out of the hot tub and calmly walked off soaking wet. Security came rushing over to intervene. Security grabbed Satin to get him to cool off. Other passengers stepped up to tell security that the guy was a problem all night, and he got what he deserved. Security calmed everything down, and the situation was under control. We left the club and went back to the cabin. We sat up and laughed after we recapped the events of the evening. Then we took it down for the night, because we had to be up early in the morning.

It was time to disembark, we were back in Florida. The captain made his announcements and calling deck by deck to get off the ship. It was finally our time to leave our cabin and line up in the hallway. Satin and I made our way up to customs. The woman called for the next person in line and stepped up. I gave her my passport and she typed in the computer. She asked me a few simple questions about the trip and handed me back my passport. She told me to proceed to the next checkpoint. Satin was next and he handed the lady his passport. She typed and then her attitude was a little more forceful with him. She asked him the purpose of the trip and a few other things and handed him his passport back. The lady told him to wait right there and someone would come to assist him. Suddenly, an officer appeared out of a side door and escorted both of us to a side room. The officer told me I had to sit outside the room on the bench. The officer took Satin into the room. As they were walking, I heard the officer ask Satin, did he pack his own luggage? Satin answered "Yes." Then the officer said, "At time did you leaved your luggage unattended?" Satin answered "No". Then the officer took him in the room and closed the door.

As passengers were cleared to get off the ship, they walked past me and stared. Everyone knew that, sitting where I was sitting, something wasn't right. I got nervous. I pulled out my phone just to look busy and kill time. Immediately, a Customs Officer approached me and told me no phones allowed, and I had to put it away. I complied and put my phone in my purse. After about an hour, the door opened and Satin came out. I could tell he was shaken up, but he tried to play it off. He took my hand and grabbed my luggage and quickly started walking out the door. We were so happy to see sunlight! We flagged down the first taxi and got in. I said, "Are you going to tell me what that was all about?" Come to find out, after scanning Satin's luggage, the machine picked up a suspicious item in his bag. After taking him in the room and physically searching his bag, customs pulled a plastic bag with a substance in it. They tested the sample, and to their surprise….it was only the beach sand from the Bahama Beach! That's when he was free to go.

We had arrived at the airport to catch our flight back to Philly. As we checked in our luggage, there was another slight problem. Satin's luggage was over the weight limit. He had to take out 12lbs or pay an extra $100!

So, we got out of the line and removed things, threw away unnecessary things, and even layered up our clothes to make the weight requirement. When we got back in line, we were fine. We were given our boarding passes, and we were off to the gate. After boarding our flight, I was relieved. The captain's voice came on over the intercom and welcomed all the passengers. He told us the flight would be on time and get ready for takeoff. While suspended in air, I replayed all the beautiful images from our vacation and just smiled. It was a vacation that was much needed. Even though we may have had a few unexpected mishaps, I enjoyed every moment.

MOTIVATION

For a while, I have been feeling like I needed change in my life. I was not happy with where I was in life and knew I could do a lot better. It was a lot of things I wanted, and I was determined to get them. The problem was I didn't know how to get started or what steps to take to reach my goals. I went to work and looked up motivational speakers to get me through the day. A black guy popped up on the screen, so I hit the button to see what he was saying. It was Les Brown. From that day forward, I could not stop listening to him. I was hooked. Hearing Les Brown's story motivated me right away to make the changes I needed in my life. I did some of the things Les had suggested by, cutting off negative people, and backing away from people content with where they were in life. My new priority was putting more time into myself. I read more to broaden my vocabulary and gain more knowledge. I enrolled in college to finish my Psychology degree I had been stopping and starting for years.   I had already been out of high school for 23 years. Things had changed drastically as far as the education curriculum. I signed up for two regular classes and one online class. I had never taken an online class before, but I thought it would be convenient.

When the semester started, I logged into my student account and saw my classmates were all chatting about the homework assignments. I didn't understand how they were chatting, and I noticed I was behind 4 homework assignments already. I emailed the professor to tell him I didn't understand how the class was chatting and I wasn't able to. I also told him I didn't receive the assignments and asked if he could help me get on track. A few hours later, I checked my email and the professor's response was unexpected. He said, Well the point of an online class is exactly that ONLINE. It is self-explanatory what to do.   I don't know what else to tell you. I read his message and was instantly furious. My temples pulsated faster and faster. My heart pounded 3 times the normal speed. The devil tried to take over and gave me several explicit words to use to respond to him. I sat at my kitchen table and cried. I thought, how could someone be so heartless to someone that needs help? The enemy kept tugging at me and telling me to give up and not to finish my semester. I was discouraged.

The enemy wanted me to throw in the towel and fail. After thinking, I called Bryan to get good, sound advice. Bryan instructed me to report the professor to the dean. Bryan explained the professor's job is to teach. His duty is to explain to his students if they need help or have questions. The professor was already paid from my tuition. After speaking with Bryan, I felt better. I gained a different outlook on the situation.

The next morning, I went to my school to speak to an advisor. I informed the advisor about the problem I was having not getting the assignments. Instantly, she said, "Oh, it sounds like your login has to be reset. I can do that for you." Within 10 minutes, my issue was solved. She allowed me to pull up the assignments in her office before I left to make sure everything was ok. I was good to go. When I left, I drove back and logged in and went to work nonstop. I caught up on the missing homework and forwarded it to the professor. His nasty attitude gave me the motivation to excel. I interacted with my classmates and participated in the discussions online. At the end of the semester, I finished the class with an A. That semester, I even made the Dean's List! Instead of cussing the professor out, I thank him for being the insensitive and uncompassionate person he was. He showed me the best revenge is massive success! So again, I thank you.

Since then, I have become a Certified Life Coach to help others in their time of need. Another thing I changed was the music I listened to. I listened to classical music, Beethoven, Bach, and Mozart. I noticed the positivity it put in my spirit. It was funny, when I would pull up at the grocery store blasting Beethoven's Fur Elise. Everyone would look at me crazy and I loved it. I also listened to Earl Nightingale, Eric Thomas, and Napoleon Hill. They made me view things in a different light. My glass was half full, instead of half empty. To obtain spiritual growth and guidance, I had to focus on my relationship with God. Next, I wrote the things, I wanted in life on the front of an index card. Then, I wrote down Matthew 7;7 -8 on the back and recited it 3 times a day. This was a necessity to claim what I wanted. I continued to eliminate the negative distractions to reach where I wanted to be. Yes, through this process, I still hit road blocks, setbacks, and disappointments. This is to be expected because things in life don't come easy. I work hard to make my children's life easier and to leave a legacy for them to carry on. As I continue to go down this road of life, I am prepared for whatever comes my way. I am ready to conquer the next chapter that life has in store for me.

DEDICATION

To my father, the late Raymond T. Logan, I miss you dearly. I will always be your "baby girl." Take comfort knowing that everything you taught me I received it and use it day to day. The example you set for me as a Man, Father, Husband, and provider will always be my standards to go by. I will continue to dance and sing to Marvin Gaye "Gotta Give It Up" and wish you were dancing with me. Until I see you again, rest easy.

Your Baby Girl

ABOUT THE AUTHOR

Adrienne Logan is a native of New Jersey. She is the mother of 3 wonderful grown children. Adrienne has dedicated 19 years of her life working for the United

States government. Realizing that she had so much more to offer, and with her passion to help others, Adrienne followed her dream. She pursued a career in counseling, and is now a Certified Life Coach while finishing up her degree in Psychology.

For her own therapy, Adrienne likes to write to express her feelings. She also enjoys exotic vacations and relaxing near beautiful water. The anticipation continues to grow for Adrienne, while she a waits the arrival of her 1st grandchild in less than 3 months!

Made in the USA
Middletown, DE
10 May 2022

65351062R00066